C000219038

Effective Fervent Prayer

Michael Kimuli

World Trumpet Mission

New Wine Press

New Wine Press
PO Box 17
Chichester PO20 6YB
United Kingdom

World Trumpet Mission
PO Box 8085
Kampala-Uganda
Tel: 256-41-232813
E-mail: trumpet@starcom.co.ug
Website: www.trumpetmission.org

All Scripture quotations are taken from the King James Version of the
Holy Bible unless otherwise indicated.

NIV – HOLY BIBLE, NEW INTERNATIONAL VERSION.
Copyright © 1973, 1978, 1984 by International Bible Society.
Used by permission.

ISBN 1 903725 16 X

Typeset by CRB Associates, Reepham, Norfolk.
Printed in England by Clays Ltd, St Ives plc.

Contents

Acknowledgements

I wish to express my appreciation to several people without whose input this book might never have become a reality.

First and foremost, I pay tribute to my pastor and mentor, John Mulinde. I am what I am today largely because of his unreserved and selfless service to my life.

Pastor Peter Odoi suggested to me that I write this book, and then helped me put down in writing the ideas and revelations God has given me on prayer. Without his contribution, this book wouldn't be out at this time. I appreciate his efforts.

My wife Sarah is a very special blessing to me. Her encouragement and support are invaluable to my work as a gospel minister. May God reward her always.

Michael Kimuli
World Trumpet Mission, Kampala

Introduction

We are living in a time when there is a bigger volume of prayer worldwide than ever before in Church history. Yet, the more prayer grows, the more people thirst and hunger for really effective ways of praying. There is a longing in many people's hearts not only to pray, but also to do so fervently and effectively.

Michael Kimuli and I have spent long hours seeking God together for this same depth. We have discovered several principles of prevailing prayer that we tested and proved effective in our lives and country, Uganda.

In this book *Effective Fervent Prayer* Michael beautifully compresses the key principles in a simple but very powerful summary that will definitely make a difference to any soul that longs to pray more effectively. This is a book for practical application. Prayer has never been easier. You are about to unveil a great secret to a deeper experience with God. I readily recommend the book.

Pastor John Mulinde
Director of World Trumpet Mission
& World Prayer-Net (Uganda)

Foreword

Persevering leadership and prevailing prayer are two of the core factors required in the transforming work of the Kingdom of God currently being experienced at both city and national levels all throughout the world.

This book by Michael Kimuli could well change your prayer life forever! He shares the keys that have been essential in seeing the extraordinary changes that have taken place in Uganda in recent years. However, these keys are available for anyone in any community, city or nation.

When used correctly, one's prayer life is dramatically changed, and ignites a passion of fervency and expectancy that will shake even a nation to its very core. In doing so, the destiny of that nation will be released, which will then become a testimony as well as a challenge to all other nations in seeking their destinies through the transforming power of effective, prevailing, fervent prayer. Are you ready for this challenge?

With your Bible at hand, read this book and you will find that your prayer life will be challenged and changed forever.

You will also be positioning your nation for an encounter with the Living God as He prepares to release His transforming power throughout society, in response to those who have chosen to stand in the gap and pay the necessary price of prayer.

It is a challenge – it is an adventure – not to be missed!

Rev. Dr. Alistair P. Petrie
Director of Sentinel Ministries
Canada
29 April 2002

Preface

Andrew Murray, renowned Christian author and Bible teacher, wrote the following words some decades ago:

> 'A man is no bigger than his prayer life. What a man is on his knees before God, that he is and nothing more. In that coming day when the hearts of men will be revealed, there will be some big men who will appear very small and those we thought to be small will turn out to be spiritual giants.'

Prayer is at the centre of any working relationship between God and man. A person's quality of spiritual life and experience is, as a rule, always directly proportional to their prayer life. No one can rise spiritually above what they are on their knees. You are equal to your prayer life.

I have read about Charles Finney, nineteenth-century American revivalist. He was well known for his strong prayer life. As a result, Finney carried the pillar of the presence of God with him wherever he went. Even when he only passed through a city or village, revival would hit that place.

I first learnt about the necessity and power of prayer from John Mulinde when I met him in 1994. At that time I was part of a home prayer group meeting in one of the suburbs of Kampala. Our group got in touch with another group meeting in a different part of the city, and on one occasion as we fellowshipped, the leader of this other group mentioned the name of John. We were talking about the men and women God has set apart for His special use in our times and this leader brought John's name as being one of such men.

A couple of days later, John visited us during our fellowship time, and as he shared his testimony, I was greatly impacted. I was so touched that I there and then renewed my covenant with God, to serve Him whole-heartedly. John visited us several other times after that, and each time he spoke to us, I sensed my spirit responding to his messages in a special way. With time I began to feel like he was to play a vital role in my spiritual destiny. At around the same time, he too sensed God leading him to pastor and father me in the things of God. We started meeting regularly for personal fellowship.

Most of the time our conversations were about prayer. Soon, I began accompanying John on his missions to different parts of Uganda.

In 1995, the Lord gave John some prophecies about

the nation. Shortly afterwards, he asked me to pray about joining him full time in the ministry. I prayed and the Lord led me to consent to John's offer. We started moving throughout Uganda, encouraging the Church to rise up and pray.

The more I worked closely with John, the more my own personal prayer life was challenged. I learnt to wake up to pray in the night and many other practical aspects of developing and maintaining a strong prayer life. My prayer life deepened.

The Lord gave John a strategy for preparing the nation for revival. It was from Genesis 12 and 13, where Abraham used altars to take Canaan, the land promised to him and his descendants. The Lord told John to use the same strategy, to 'build Me a net of prayer so that I can fish the nation out of troubled waters.'

I offered to use my home village as an experimental ground to test the strategy. My village was full of all kinds of evil: witchcraft, drunkenness, etc. There was only one church in the area, an orthodox church. I started praying in my house with my wife for the village, sometimes fasting. Soon other believers in the village joined us, and we began praying from house to house. We carried out spiritual mapping so that we could pray informed prayers. We prayed every day.

After some time, changes started happening. Witchcraft shrines began to be closed down. New churches were planted. My Dad visited one day to warn me that the spiritualists in the village were complaining about our prayers. The experience proved that the strategy was working. Personally, I was very encouraged by the power of prayer to change things. My prayer life was deepened further.

I became bolder in encouraging people to pray for their communities around the country. In places that were hard, we taught the people not to give up but to increase the volume of prayer. I now knew how to pray to the level of breakthrough. I had learnt the need to persevere in prayer.

I am aware that almost every average Christian tries to pray, at least once in a while. What I've written here, however, is not about the 'regular' kind of praying. I am speaking about breakthrough praying: the kind of praying where you know that you feel and touch and experience God on a regular basis. I am talking about how Christians can learn to enjoy staying in the presence of God early and long. I am showing how God's people can cause revival to happen in their individual lives, families and nations through the power of effective fervent prayer.

I am confident that everyone who reads this book to the end will not remain the same. They will be fired up to pray like they have never thought possible. They will begin to enjoy spending time with the Father. They will experience tremendous breakthroughs.

Sometime ago the Lord spoke to us in Uganda that He has called us to be a prayer missionary nation, and that wherever we would go and whenever we would minister, we would be able to impart the spirit of prayer, of grace and supplication, to others. That impartation will happen in the life of everyone who reads and takes to heart what is written here.

Michael Kimuli
World Trumpet Mission
Kampala

Chapter 1

Why Prayer?

Jeremiah 29:12–13 says,

> *'Then shall ye call upon me, and ye shall go and pray
> unto me, and I will hearken unto you. And ye shall seek
> me and find me, when ye shall search for me with all
> your heart.'*

This is only one of the numerous scriptures in the Bible
in which God specifically invites His people to pray to
Him. We know that prayer is worthwhile and profitable
because of the way God speaks about it. Over and over
again, we are encouraged and even commanded to seek
God. There is no doubt that prayer is a vital aspect of a
victorious Christian life.

What prayer is

In this book we shall explore the dynamics of effective prayer but first we need to define prayer itself. What does it mean to pray as taught in the Bible?

Simply put, prayer is the means by which we as people come into partnership with God in order to bring God's will to come to pass on earth. Prayer is declaring the will of God on earth.

Prayer is partnership with God because true prayer is a two-way communication. It is a dialogue between God and man, not a monologue. Prayer involves man speaking to God and God speaking to man; man pouring out his heart to God as God too pours out His heart to man.

A lot of times people go to God to give Him counsel and they call that prayer. They go and advise God about what they want Him to do about their situations. They approach God as though He has no idea whatsoever about what they are saying and so they inform Him about what is taking place and what the solutions are. After they are through 'counselling' God, they take off, never waiting to listen to what God has to say.

Mathew 6:32 says,

> '. . . [the] *heavenly Father knoweth that ye have need of all these things.'*

Before we even start telling God all our stuff, He already knows. In prayer we bring nothing new to God's attention. That is why we do not have to merely inform Him about our situations and then run away.

Someone might ask that if God knows everything before we even open our mouths to speak to Him, why then should we even bother praying at all? Because God needs our partnership and co-operation if He is to have His will and purpose happen on earth as well as in our individual lives.

We are fallen

We are a fallen people. We have a sinful and fallen nature within us. As a result, everything within us responds easier to the devil than to God. Even after we commit our lives to the Lord, there are things within us which keep trying to pull us back into darkness.

Prayer is the means by which we deny and divorce ourselves from those parts of us which tend towards darkness. Through prayer, we commit and re-commit again and again the whole of ourselves to God, thus pulling ourselves away from the sinful and fallen tendencies towards fulfilling God's will and purposes.

As we focus on God in prayer with a yielding heart, we come out with the evil desires within us broken. As we interact with God, we discover that our opinions conflict with God's; our intentions, plans, agendas are all wrong. We discover that we must change if we are to see God's purposes and plans come to pass.

Legal ground

Prayer gives God the legal ground to act on our behalf.

Genesis 6:3 declares that *'My spirit shall not always strive with man.'* God will not compel man to do His will. God will not force man to do what he (man) isn't willing to do. God will never violate man's will. In prayer, we yield to God and thus give Him the legal basis upon which He can act to meet our needs.

Yes, it is true that God does good even to the wicked, to those who never pray. Luke 6:35 says,

> *'...he is kind unto the unthankful and to the evil.'*

However, it is also true that there are times when God waits for us, the believers, to come and commune with Him before He acts.

In Isaiah 1:18 God invites us to come and reason with Him, promising that even if our sins are as red as crimson, they will be as white as snow. He promises in the next verse, 19, that if we are willing and obedient to walk in partnership with Him, we shall eat the good of the land. You see, people of God, as we present our case to God and He too presents His case to us – reasoning together – we discover that most of our reasoning is contrary to God's will. The result is that we yield to God's will (reason) through repentance and broken-heartedness.

Key to strong relationship

Not to have a prayer life is missing out on partnership with the Almighty God, something that is very dangerous.

Prayerlessness means we are depending on our own understanding, our own plans, and our own limited insight into the future.

Prayer is communicating with God and, as we all know, communication is what keeps relationships strong. No marriage, for example, can succeed without good communication. Husband and wife cannot stay closed to each other and still hope to make it. They have to open up.

The quality of communication determines the depth of any relationship. People of God, there is absolutely no way a prayerless Christian can have a great relationship with God. I see many Christians to whom prayer is at the very bottom of priorities and I wonder how they expect to walk with the Father. People, things simply do not work that way.

Satan hates prayer

Ephesians 6:10–12 commands us to be strong in the Lord and in the power of His might because,

> '... we wrestle not against flesh and blood, but against principalities, against powers, against the rulers of the darkness of this world, against spiritual wickedness in high places.'

The believer's enemy is not physical and therefore cannot be fought with physical weapons. He can only be attacked spiritually. Prayer is one of the major spiritual weapons we have available for us.

Prayer is lethal to the devil and so he hates it. The devil doesn't want to see any church or individual engaging in effective prayer. Hordes of demons are constantly working to weaken the prayer lives of God's people, to cover them with blankets of prayerlessness.

The devil knows that if he can succeed in making God's people prayerless, he will then have free rein to work his evil in the nations, families, and local churches as well as in individual lives.

Every time we pray, Satan loses. He gets heart attacks. We need to give him those heart attacks continually!

Godly priesthood versus satanic priesthood

God is calling His people to learn to pray to levels where they experience breakthroughs. I strongly believe that the prophetic words spoken in Isaiah 11:9 are about come to pass literally:

> *'They shall not hurt nor destroy in all my holy moun-tain: for the earth shall be full of the knowledge of the LORD, as the waters cover the sea.'*

I believe that we are about to experience breakthroughs that have never been imagined possible. The kingdom of God will win.

But before this will happen, God's people have to take their place in effective prayer as people of God, rising up as priests before Him in every city, nation and community. God always raises a godly priesthood. God raises His people to intercede for that city, nation or community. On the other side, the devil also raises his own satanic priesthood who serve at his altar, whose job is to counteract what the godly priesthood are assigned to do.

In Africa it is quite easy to identify the sites of satanic priesthood. Satan's servants openly identify themselves by their shrines, their titles – witch-doctors, etc. If anyone wants to find concentrations of satanic priest-hoods, it is quite simple to know where to go. In the West, it isn't always easy to recognise the devil's assis-tants. The devil's shrines are just as nicely built as any other buildings, unlike in Africa where they are peculiar: little grass-thatched huts with unique paraphernalia within them. Some people have thought that in the West there are no satanic priesthoods because they aren't easily identifiable. That isn't true. There are just as many satanic priesthoods in the cities of the developed nations as there are in the third world, and they are equally active!

In the book of the Acts of the Apostles, chapter 8, the Bible mentions a satanic priest called Simon who had manipulated and intimidated the citizens of the city of Samaria for a long time. The stronghold of that city was sorcery. The people had all been awed and completely taken up by the manifestations of Satan's power as it revealed itself through Simon.

That was until Philip hit the city!

Philip was a deacon from the church in Jerusalem. He wasn't an apostle or a pastor, just a deacon but with the pillar of God's presence accompanying him wherever he went. When he started ministering in the city, Satan's power was exposed as being far inferior to God's. Within a few days, the satanic hold over the city was in ruins. Even Simon the sorcerer himself was convinced, and for a time, became part of Philip's meetings.

People, if one man could challenge and expose the frailty of the devil's power in a city like that, what can two or three people accomplish? It is possible!

I have a feeling that God is right now anointing the Church to do combat with the enemy and destroy his hold over cities and nations. It happened in Samaria. It is going to happen many times over in the cities and nations of our times! In many areas, satanic priesthoods are more honoured than godly priesthoods. Witch-doctors are held in higher esteem than pastors and other spiritual leaders. But let me prophesy to you: that is about to end!

Don't limit God

I have heard some believers express despair because of the evil Satan is perpetrating right now on earth. They feel that there is no use trying to pray anymore because wickedness is simply too much. They ask: What will it help praying when evils like homosexuality and abortion have been legalised by the governments of the nations? What can we, insignificant churches, do in the face of such determination by the nations to disregard God's laws?

My answer to that is: we serve the Almighty God! His throne is in heaven and the earth is His footstool. All the nations put together are as a drop of water in His presence. We serve a powerful God. And not only is He powerful, He is the power itself! Nothing is impossible to Him!

We must never limit our God. It is wrong for God's people to focus so much on the evil in the world that we lose the burden to pray. Yes, things are bad and are getting worse every day, but that is only one side of the story. The other side is that God is very much in charge and His power to save, deliver and turn around situations has not diminished one inch!

It is possible for us in our own lifetime to see God's will done on earth. We must pray. We must seek God. We have to arise and call upon God until He establishes our cities and nations and makes them praises on earth. It is possible!

Personal victory

Jeremiah 29:11 says,

> *'For I know the thoughts that I think toward you, saith the LORD, thoughts of peace, and not of evil, to give you an expected end.'*

God has a plan and purpose for each one of us. His thoughts toward you as an individual are to give you a hope and a future. He means good towards you.

A lot of times we fail to see things the way God sees. It would help us to remember that God knows us from beginning to end. He knows what is best for us. God has a hand in whatever circumstances we handle. He has the right version of what every situation is supposed to be.

God calls upon us to pray because He knows us so well, and too, He has our very best interests at heart. He wants us to seek for His grace, His help, and His assistance because He knows we need them in order to make it in our lives. We ought to pay more attention to prayer because it helps bring us into God's will and purpose for our lives. God has promised that if we shall pray, He will listen and cause to come to pass what He has in His heart for us.

Prayer should not be drudgery for us. We should be eager to pray. It is for our own good and for the good of those we love and care about. The Lord Jesus told His disciples in Luke 22:40: *'Pray that ye enter not into temptation.'* Defeat isn't far from us as long as our prayer life isn't what it should be. God loves us and wants the best for us but His will doesn't happen automatically. The disciples didn't take heed to the Lord's admonition and a short while later they experienced terrible defeat. They so backslid that when the Lord appeared to them after His resurrection, Peter couldn't even recognize Him at first. He who had vehemently vowed never to deny the Lord so reverted back to his former profession of fishing that he could not recognise Jesus as He stood by the seashore until John told him, 'It is the Lord'. If Peter and the others had prayed through when the Lord told them to, they would not have gone through such defeat and embarrassment.

We must pray. If the disciples, the great forefathers of Christianity needed to stay prayed-up in order to live in victory, we do not need anything less.

Chapter 2

Asking:
First Level of Prayer

According to Luke 11:1–13, the disciples asked the Lord Jesus to teach them to pray. In response the Lord taught them what is commonly known as the Lord's Prayer.

The Lord presented this prayer as a pattern the disciples were to follow in their own corporate as well as individual praying. He didn't tell them that they were to 'say' the prayer word for word and nothing else each time they prayed but were to use it as a model or a guideline. Matthew's account of the same incident brings out this point more clearly. According to Matthew 6:9, the Lord said, *'After this manner therefore pray ye...'* Note the words 'after this manner': following this pattern; according to this guideline.

In this pattern given in the Lord's Prayer, we learn that there are different types of prayer. (Ephesians 6:18 speaks of praying with different kinds of prayer.) They are:

1. **Fellowship** – Our Father who art in heaven

2. **Praise** – Hallowed be Thy Name

3. **Intercession** – Thy kingdom come, Thy will be done on earth as in heaven

4. **Petition** – Give us this day our daily bread

5. **Repentance** – And forgive us our trespasses

6. **Deliverance** – Lead us not into temptation but deliver us from evil

7. **Worship and thanksgiving** – For thine is the kingdom, the power and the glory forever, Amen.

After giving the pattern for prayer, the Lord went on to teach the disciples about the importance of persistence in prayer (Luke 11:5–8). We shall deal in detail with the subject of persistence later. Then the Lord spoke certain words in verses 9 and 10 concerning prayer that are my main interest now:

'And I say unto you, Ask, and it shall be given you; seek, and ye shall find; knock, and it shall be opened unto you. For every one that asketh receiveth; and he that seeketh findeth; and to him that knocketh it shall be opened.'

In these words the Lord taught about what I refer to as the three levels of prayer. The first is the asking level of prayer; the second is the seeking level; and the third is the knocking level. Each of these levels of prayer is different from the others and is a necessary part of effective prayer. In this chapter we shall explore the dynamics of the first level. The next two chapters will focus on the other two levels.

Asking

'Ask, and it shall be given you.' Asking is the starting point in effective prayer. Prayer is like climbing a hill. You begin at the bottom and then work your way up towards the top. Asking is at the bottom of the prayer hill, so to speak.

Asking is what is known as petition prayer. You make requests concerning specific things or issues. This is the kind of prayer spoken about in Philippians 4:6:

> *'Be careful for nothing; but in every thing by prayer and supplication with thanksgiving let your requests be made known unto God.'*

At this level, you know what you want to say to God. You might have a written list of particular things or issues you want God to deal with. You know exactly what you want to get from God. Asking is the 'known' level of prayer.

29

Effective petitioning

In all prayer it is possible to come out with absolutely nothing. There are qualities that make our prayers effective, that guarantee results as we make requests to God. Below are the qualities that effective petitioning must have:

1.   Asking in faith

    'And all things, whatsoever ye shall ask in prayer, believing, ye shall receive.'   (Mathew 21:22)

2.   Abiding in a vibrant, strong relationship with the Lord

    'If ye abide in me, and my words abide in you, ye shall ask what ye will, and it shall be done unto you.'
                                             (John 15:7)

3.   Right motives – holiness contributes greatly to the effectiveness of your asking

    'If I regard iniquity in my heart, the Lord will not hear me.'   (Psalm 66:18)

4.   Asking in accordance with God's will

    'And this is the confidence that we have in him, that, if we ask anything according to his will, he heareth us. And if we know that he hear us, whatsoever we ask, we know that we have the petitions that we desired of him.'   (1 John 5:14–15)

5. Being specific when asking – Romans 4:17–25

6. Delighting in the Lord

   'Delight thyself also in the Lord; and he shall give thee the desires of thine heart.'   (Psalm 37:4)

7. Basing your prayer on the promises of God

8. Living right

   'Ye ask, and receive not, because ye ask amiss, that ye may consume it upon your lusts.'   (James 4:3)

Asking is in the mind

The asking level of prayer is basically in the mind. Most of the time, the spirit of a person is not involved. As I said, in asking you know in your head what you want to get from God. There is no need to wait upon God to illuminate your mind about His will in the situation. You have your desires and you request God to grant them. In the asking level, man is speaking to God almost all of the time.

While this level of prayer is important, it is basically done in the flesh, in the natural. Someone who stops at the asking level never gets to really enter into the presence of God, into fellowship with God.

Petitioning God for things is not seeking Him, as so many people think. This has to do with you, out of your mind and out of your circumstances, going to God and requesting that He intervenes. And yes, God has promised to grant our requests. He encourages us to ask. But we have to note that this level of prayer is basically one-sided, a monologue. I pointed out in the previous chapter that, in the final analysis, true prayer is a dialogue. This therefore means that we should never stop at the asking level if we really desire to pray. We should proceed to the next level: the seeking level.

The asking level usually has the danger of repetition. You have your list and after a few minutes in prayer, you find that you have exhausted the list. And so you begin afresh going through the list because you wish to spend a little more time in prayer. After a while you are again through with the list and you go back to item number one. When you begin to experience this tendency to repeat yourself in this manner, that is the time to drop that list and go on into seeking God.

Chapter 3

Seeking:
Second Level of Prayer

Psalm 42:1–3 says,

> 'As the hart panteth after the water brooks, so panteth
> my soul after thee, O God. My soul thirsteth for God, for
> the living God: when shall I come and appear before
> God? My tears have been my meat day and night, while
> they continually say to me, "Where is thy God?"'

This passage of Scripture expresses the very essence of
the seeking level of prayer.

   As you press on in prayer, you come to a level where
you get out of praying out of your mind. You step into a

higher dimension. When you come to the end of the asking level, running out of words because your list of items have all been presented to God, maybe several times, you are now ready to begin seeking. That is not the time to quit. When you no longer have anything in your mind to tell God, you don't have to stop praying. That is the time to progress to a deeper level. So many people miss out on God's best because they quit after the asking level.

Praying out of the heart

You see, when you are through praying out of your mind, out of the flesh, out of the natural, you are now ready to begin praying out of your heart. Your inner man takes over and you begin crying to God from within. At this time you aren't concerned about 'things' or circumstances. You are now in a position to let your heart begin expressing its desire for communion with God. Deep is calling unto deep here. You find yourself saying words like, 'I need You God. I desire You.' You are no longer bothered about your natural needs. You now want God Himself.

Hunger

At the asking level of prayer, there are struggles with such things as wandering thoughts, lack of concentration, etc. because everything is being done in the flesh.

34

As one enters the seeking level, however, it is the soul, the inner man, that gets involved and God takes over the praying. A hunger develops for more of God, more of spiritual realities. This hunger now becomes the driving force behind the prayer from that point on. A breakthrough into the spirit realm is experienced. A flow develops. The desire to quit praying ends. The compelling desire in the praying person is now to touch God, to feel Him, to experience the reality of the presence of the Father. A yearning, a deep longing for God, is the driving force behind the prayer, not desires to have God provide material things, etc.

Oh how beautiful prayer becomes when you break through to the seeking level! Oh how sweet it is to reach a level in prayer where you no longer bother about time! All you want is God. Not things. Not God solving your problems. You want God Himself. That's hunger!

People of God, we can all break through to this level if only we can learn to stay a little longer on our knees. The longer we stay in prayer, the closer we get to God.

Too many people give up too soon. Day after day they never experience breakthroughs into the spirit realm.

They wonder why they are always so dry during prayer, why they never develop any hunger for God. The problem is that they stop at the asking level. Once they have asked God for things, they end right there. People, there is a deeper realm. There is a place where you can begin to enjoy prayer, to enjoy God.

God takes over

At the seeking level, God Himself takes over. This is the point in prayer where Romans 8:26 becomes practical:

> *'Likewise the Spirit also helpeth our infirmities: for we know not what we should pray for as we ought: but the Spirit itself maketh intercession for us with groanings that cannot be uttered.'*

As I have already mentioned several times, at the asking level it is you telling God your stuff out of your mind as you see the situation. At the seeking level, it is the hunger for deeper intimacy with God driving you to pray on. At this level your soul is reaching out to God and the Lord Himself begins helping you – giving you the words to speak. You do not know the adequate words to express your true feelings. So the Spirit takes over and helps you express the deep longings of your heart. You and God become partners in prayer. It is no longer just you talking to God in your own strength and wisdom.

The hunger that drives us to seek God is not something we can work up on our own. It is God who pours it out upon us. It isn't something man-made. So you see that unless God has taken over your praying that hunger may not be there. But God can't take over unless you are willing to spend enough time in His presence.

Sighs, tears

As God takes over your praying, helping you express the hunger and yearning of your soul, sometimes all that you will do is sigh deeply. Often you will find that you break into tears. Weeping is one of the most common methods of releasing that deep hunger and yearning within. Tears become a good medium of communication. All of us need to get to that place where only tears speak, at least once in a while. I tell you when God truly touches people, you will find even so-called 'strong' men weeping like babies. In prayer God doesn't hear prayers only; He sees tears as well.

> 'Go back and tell Hezekiah, the leader of my people, "This is what the LORD, the God of your father David says: I have heard your prayers and seen your tears; I will heal you."' (2 Kings 20:5, NIV)

Tongues

In 1 Corinthians 14:2, we are told that

> '...he that speaketh in an unknown tongue speaketh not unto men, but unto God: for no man understandeth him; howbeit in the spirit he speaketh mysteries.'

One way to break through to the seeking level is to begin speaking in tongues. When you feel that you have no more words in your head to tell God, move on into tongues. Unlike praying out of the mind, praying in tongues can go on and on for a long time.

Praying in tongues is one of the most effective types of prayer. First of all, it gets the devil totally confused. Satan can't understand a thing when we pray in tongues. He is completely out of the picture, totally outclassed. Not only don't men understand us when we talk in tongues but the entire kingdom of demons is in black-out! It is only God who understands tongues, and those to whom God reveals. We speak mysteries to God. 1 Corinthians 14 teaches that there are different kinds of tongues. There are tongues which can be interpreted into a regular or known language. This kind is used in prophesying. Then there are tongues which are actually known languages but foreign to the persons who speak the words. This kind of tongues happened on the day of Pentecost as recorded in Acts 2. People from different areas heard Judeans speak in their languages and yet they were sure that the Judeans didn't previously know the languages.

People, we need the gifts of the Spirit in the Church. Some of my readers might be sceptical about the gifts of the Spirit but I can tell you that there are times when nothing else will do.

So tongues can be used for different purposes as the Lord wills but my interest right now is using tongues as a prayer language. This is something available to all believers and it is so helpful in seeking God.

Seek Christ

Solomon wrote the following words in the Song of Songs 1:4:

> '*Draw me, we will run after thee: the king hath brought me into his chambers: we will be glad and rejoice in thee, we will remember thy love more than wine; the upright love thee.*'

Seeking God is responding to His gentle call to enter His chambers, His secret places, His innermost sanctuary.

> '*O God, thou art my God; early will I seek thee: my soul thirsteth for thee, my flesh longeth for thee in a dry and thirsty land, where no water is; To see thy power and thy glory, so as I have seen thee in the sanctuary.*'
>
> (Psalm 63:1–2)

Always remember that when you go beyond wanting God to merely give you things, perform miracles to meet your needs, etc., although there's nothing wrong with that, you are beginning to seek Him. You are seeking for His presence, His knowledge. You want to know Him better. You want to walk with Him.

It is at this point that you begin to die to the flesh and to the desires and lusts of the world. Things that have been exciting you and meaning so much to you begin to lose their appeal. All you want is God. You want to know the mystery of God in Christ. You now realize that only more of Jesus can satisfy you.

- Don't seek deliverance, seek Christ – He is the Deliverer

- Don't seek benefits, seek Christ – He is the Benefactor

- Don't seek power, seek Christ – He is the Power

- Don't seek wisdom, seek Christ – He is the Wisdom

- Don't seek healing, seek Christ – He is the Healer

We would find most of the things we seek for sooner if only we focused on seeking Christ rather than concentrating on the things. Proverbs 8:35 says,

'For whoso findeth me findeth life, and shall obtain favour of the LORD.'

If and when you find Christ, you find everything.

Seek and you will find. That is speaking about pressing on further to greater intimacy with the Father. Nowhere in Scripture are we told to seek for things but throughout the Bible there are admonitions to seek God. It is a higher dimension of prayer. We must all get into that dimension. It is the will of God.

Chapter 4

Knocking:
Third Level of Prayer

Some people think that just any kind of praying is seeking God. No! No! In seeking the focus and emphasis is on Christ. That is why praise and worship are so natural at this point. As you gaze at the Lord, you find yourself adoring Him, loving Him, prostrating yourself before Him. And it is all so natural. The main issue is Him.

The knocking level of prayer is the highest of all three. This is the level where you enter heart to heart communion with the Father. At this level, you are not asking or even seeking God. Now you are in the very inner corridors of God's presence and He shares His heart and burdens with you. You become one with God, a partner in a very real sense.

Moses' tabernacle – prayer journey

Effective fervent prayer or breakthrough prayer is a journey: from praying in the natural, to praying out of the soul, to the climax – praying out of the spirit. Asking is out of the mind – natural; seeking is out of the soul, while knocking is out of the spirit.

The tabernacle constructed by Moses in the wilderness of Sinai had three courts: the outer court, the inner court (holy place) and the innermost court (holy of holies). Those three courts correspond to the three levels in the prayer journey. I call the asking level outer court prayer. You are in the courtyard of God's presence but not in the very presence. You know that God's presence is shut up in the holy of holies but you aren't there. So you pray but do not experience or feel the presence of God.

The seeking level corresponds to the inner court, the holy place, which had a lamp and the table of show-bread. The lamp represents revelation. At the seeking level, you gain insight into the things of God. You see more clearly your need for God. You develop a hunger for the presence of God but you are not yet experiencing it in full. You are close but you aren't there. You need to keep going. This is inner court praying.

It is only when you break through the veil to the holy of holies that you are face to face with God. That corresponds to the knocking level – innermost court prayer.

People, we shouldn't spend our entire lives in the outer court – merely knowing that there is such a thing as the possibility of getting into the presence of God but never doing so ourselves. Neither should we settle down in the inner court. We must never give up until we are sure that we are regularly meeting with God face to face. Nothing can be substituted for that.

Carried along by the Spirit

At the seeking level the Holy Spirit helps us to express the yearnings of our hearts but this help intensifies as we enter the knocking level. It is deeper. Here the Holy Spirit begins bearing witness with our spirits (Romans 8:16). The Divine Spirit and the human spirit become so fused together that actually the Spirit isn't just helping us cry to God but is Himself praying through us. The Holy Spirit carries us along. The Spirit begins to intercede through us.

You see, the Holy Spirit needs us to accomplish His intercessory ministry. That is the essence of the message in Romans 8:26–27:

> 'Likewise the Spirit also helpeth our infirmities: for we know not what we should pray for as we ought: but the Spirit itself maketh intercession for us with groanings which cannot be uttered. And he that searcheth the hearts knoweth what is the mind of the Spirit, because he maketh intercession for the saints according to the will of God'.

True intercession

As the Holy Spirit literally takes over the praying, you

43

begin to feel as God feels. There is an impartation that happens. You begin to see things from God's viewpoint. You begin to feel for people as God feels for them and then you begin to cry on their behalf.

- The Father desires to think through our thoughts;

- He wants to feel through our hearts;

- He wants to speak through our lips;

- He wants to weep through our eyes;

- He wants to groan through our spirits.

There is absolutely no intercession at the asking level. There you are concerned with your needs and your circumstances. Even at the seeking level there is not much intercession. You are desiring to satisfy your own hunger for more of God. But at the knocking level, you turn your attention to the burdens of God's heart. You begin to reach out to those beyond you.

You cannot stay in the presence of God and continue to be indifferent to the needs of the people around you. Intercession is born out of intimacy with God. True intercession is not man-made or man-initiated. The ordinary human being is so selfish that he/she cannot by him/herself develop a real burden for others. That is why so few Christians really intercede for others. How can they when they hardly ever break through into the presence of God, where they can feel for others as God does? Any one who wants to be an intercessor has to be able to stay long enough before God to regularly enter or even perpetually stay in that presence.

God speaks

At the asking level, man speaks to God; at the seeking level, man cries to God driven by the hunger in his soul; but at the knocking level, God begins speaking to man; communion takes place.

Now I know that some people believe that God no longer speaks to man directly. Well, from my personal experience and from the teaching of Scripture, I know that that isn't true. The Word of God clearly says that God doesn't change. He is the same yesterday, today and for ever (Hebrews 13:8). If He spoke in the past, and He doesn't change, then He speaks today as well. Many who say that God no longer speaks have simply never learnt to get to that place where God can speak to them.

Our God is not a statue, a mute idol. He isn't a Buddha. He is a Living Being. He speaks back if we press on into His presence. When we get near enough to Him, we begin to hear His voice, to see His glory.

There are times when nothing will do except God speaking. I remember one time when we went somewhere to minister but we couldn't get a breakthrough. There was resistance to our ministry. We were praying as we had always done – for one, two hours sometimes – but we were clearly losing the battle. We then knew that we needed to hear from God if we were going to make any headway. So we set time to seek God, and for some eight hours, we called upon God non-stop. Finally there was a breakthrough. One of us received a vision showing what the problem was. We dealt with the problem and had great meetings from then on.

Staying long

People of God, it is important to stay long enough in the presence of God for Him to speak. We have to pray until we get into the spirit. God does not speak when we are still in the flesh.

Some of us behave like a little child who goes to his father to ask for something but then runs out of the room before the father responds to his request. They are too much in a hurry to leave. They pray according to their schedules. They in effect tell God things like, 'Hey God, I've got only thirty minutes to spare for You. Speak quickly or else I will be gone.'

Friends, you can't fix God in your schedule. Instead you have to let Him fix you in His schedule. I hear people say stuff like, 'I am going to separate myself and seek God for three days.' My question is, how do you know whether you will find Him in three days? You do not control the timing. He does! Sometimes, He may be found in thirty minutes, other times in five days or even weeks!

Moses went up the mountain and spent forty days. God did not particularly instruct him to be there for forty days but Moses knew that he needed to stay there long enough for God to speak, whatever period that would be. He was willing to be fixed on God's time-table.

To experience regular breakthroughs in prayer, you have to lose time consciousness. Throw timing prayer out of the window. Stay before God for as long as He wants you there. And always remember something I've already mentioned elsewhere: the longer you stay, the closer you get; the longer you stay, the more ground you gain. And the closer you get, the hungrier you become!

There is something people do when they fail to wait long enough for God to speak. After a few minutes of outer court prayer, they close their eyes, blindly open their Bibles and stick a finger on whatever page falls open. They then read whatever scripture they find their finger on, claiming that whatever that scripture says is what God is telling them. That is so pathetic. It actually isn't anything less than fortune telling. Any witch-doctor can do that. It doesn't take any spiritual effort to open scriptures like that.

We must learn to stay long enough in prayer to hear the actual voice of God. You can reach a place in prayer where you are so confident of God speaking to you that you are able to stand and tell the whole nation, 'This is what God is saying.' You know that you have heard from God. And you know that what you are saying is going to come to pass. But if you prophesy things out of your own mind, they won't take place and then everyone will know that you were telling lies out of your own mind.

Inhaling God

The knocking level of prayer is so sweet. The things of this world totally lose their glamour and attraction. At this level God shows you His glory and you become a changed person.

According to Exodus 33:7–22, Moses spent time seeking God on behalf of the people he was leading. At some point in his communion with God, he got so consumed with the desire to experience the glory of God that he prayed, *'Show me Your glory.'* In response, the Lord hid him in a cleft of a rock and then let His glory pass by. Moses literally saw the form of God!

After that encounter, Moses became a new man. As he came down from Mount Sinai, his face was radiant with the glory of God. He had spoken with God! He had seen God face to face!

When you meet God in His sanctuary, in the holy of holies, He clothes you with His glory. You exhale yourself and you inhale God!

Total satisfaction

Beloved of God, there is such a thing as face-to-face encounter with the Father! And you know what, in that encounter, all that human beings long for is abundantly supplied! In that place man becomes whole. The vacuum within gets filled. So many people, including born again people, are empty within but they think that that vacuum can be filled by material success, etc. Oh no!

Only the manifest presence of God can take away the emptiness. And when that happens, all the rest falls into place. You see, God always works from the inside out. He begins dealing first with the heart and then works His way to the outer parts of us. If a person is empty within, he/she cannot be fulfilled without.

Silence

The knocking level of prayer is spirit to Spirit. A lot of times this communion is so deep that it cannot be expressed in audible or even intelligible words. It is silence that prevails, and yet what sweet fellowship goes on! Other times it is tears, silent tears! Silent tears can mean a lot more than words. It is the unseen human spirit communing with the unseen Spirit of God. This is the height of fellowship. A heart cry without words is far more desirable than loud words without heart!

In the holy of holies there was silence. God was there! God was in control! The high priest who alone was permitted to enter there once a year was not to speak.

When Moses went to Mount Sinai to meet with God and the glory of God passed by him, he didn't speak again. He had seen God; what more could he say? He didn't need to ask any more questions. He now understood. When God speaks, you need not ask anything any more! One word from God can change a person's life for ever. That one word will be remembered by that person for the rest of their life. God's voice is not like man's. That is why if God ever speaks to a person, they will want to go back again and again to that level of fellowship where God spoke to them.

God's desire for fellowship

Man was created to fellowship with God. Man was created to dwell perpetually in the presence of God. And the Scriptures show that God too longs for fellowship with man. God is a Living Spirit (John 4:24). He seeks for worshippers. What that means is that He seeks for people to fellowship with. When Adam and Eve sinned against God and hid from His presence, God came asking, *'Where art thou?'* God has always been running after us, wanting to commune with us.

So man needs fellowship with God and God too desires fellowship with man but this fellowship cannot happen unless man presses on in prayer, past his flesh and natural tendencies, to the place where God resides and manifests. It is possible. It can be done. We need it. We must pursue it.

Chapter 5

Hindrances
to a Strong Prayer Life

Prayer has enemies. The job of these enemies is to hinder the people of God from praying through to victory, or even worse, hinder them from getting started in prayer at all. Most of God's people have an inner desire to commune with the Father but they find themselves unable and they wonder why. The enemies are at work. In this chapter I expose the most common of these enemies and show how to deal with them.

Hindrance 1: *Lack of righteousness*

> *'The effectual fervent prayer of a righteous man availeth much.'* (James 5:16b)

Effective prayer comes out of a righteous heart. The person who would pray must have a pure and clean heart before God. He/she must be right with God.

> *'If I regard iniquity in my heart, the Lord will not hear me.'*   (Psalm 66:18)

Sin mightily affects our prayer life. Isaiah 59:2 teaches that sin separates us from God. Since that is so, there is no way we can speak of breaking through in prayer with sin in our lives. We are already separated even before we begin to pray.

Psalm 34:15–16 says that

> *'The eyes of the L*ORD *are upon the righteous, and his ears are open unto their cry. The face of the L*ORD *is against them that do evil, to cut off the remembrance of them from the earth.'*

What I want you to note here is that righteousness and holiness contribute to the effectiveness of prayer.

Hindrance 2: *Loss of first love*

> *'And them that are turned back from the L*ORD*; and those that have not sought the L*ORD*, nor enquired of him.'*   (Zephaniah 1:6)

The second hindrance to a strong prayer life is turning

back from following the Lord wholeheartedly, from loving the Lord above all things.

Usually when people first come to the Lord, there is that first love. There is a fire, a desire to serve God. They want to win souls to the Lord, to be filled with the Holy Spirit, to attend every prayer meeting, to learn the meaning of every scripture. They stop associating closely with the ungodly. A lot of things change. As time goes on, however, the converts meet others who have been saved longer and the old believers begin telling them that their fire is temporary, that soon they will lose that zeal. The old Christians tell the new ones that they were also once on fire like that but they cooled down to a more 'normal' Christian life; they 'parked' in a place of 'normal' saved life. And so the new believers too begin to lose that first love and eventually park where the old ones have parked: no zeal, prayerlessness, and lukewarmness.

Beloved, the attitude that zeal for God is for new believers kills a prayer life. It leads to compromise with the world. It leads to going back to the same kind of lifestyle of the ungodly. There is no way you can go back to the old lifestyle and still maintain a strong prayer life. The two simply don't mesh.

Right atmosphere

In order to be effective in prayer, you have got to create the right atmosphere around your everyday life. At my house, for example, I don't permit anyone to watch ungodly TV programmes or listen to the junk being broadcast on most of the radio frequencies. As the head of my family I have set the rules. You see, I need the presence of God at my house. I can't have that, however, if devil-like tunes keep blaring away through the loud speakers of our music systems. Devil-like tunes and pictures attract demons, not the manifest presence of God.

You cannot spend your days reading gossip columns of newspapers and other pornographic stuff and still have a desire to spend much time with God. You can't spend hours in ungodly chatter and still maintain a strong love for Jesus.

We must stop familiarizing the Lord. People get so used to being Christians that they actually stop living like one. If you lose that first love and revert back to the old lifestyle, the Christ-life begins to decrease in you as the strength of your own human life, your flesh, increases.

It is up to you to avoid losing your first love. In fact, love for things of God should increase, not decrease with time. But it all depends on what kind of atmosphere you live and walk in. If you feel that you have lost your first love, you need to repent right now and determine to get back to where you are supposed to be with God. Ask God to restore to you that first love.

> *'Yet I hold this against you: You have forsaken your first love. Remember the height from which you have fallen! Repent and do the things you did at first. If you do not repent, I will come to you and remove your lampstand from its place.'*   (Revelation 2:4–5, NIV)

Hindrance 3: *Lack of fear of God*

> *'Yea, thou castest off fear, and restrainest prayer before God.'* (Job 15:4)

Reverencing God or fearing Him is essential to maintaining a healthy prayer life. When we cast off the fear of God, our prayer life is automatically restrained. Absence of fear of God automatically means absence of prayer life.

You can't really seek a God you don't reverence. Without that reverence you are apt to live like a non-believer, like it or not. And you know that non-believers don't pray. When the fear of God leaves, your prayer life dies.

Cultivate a healthy fear for God. Never take things of God for granted. Your view of God can determine the difference between life and death. Take care how you rate God.

Hindrance 4: *Not delighting in the Lord*

> *'Will he delight himself in the Almighty? Will he always call upon God?'* (Job 27:10)

To delight in God means to rejoice in Him, to praise Him, to worship Him, regardless of circumstances. A person who makes it a habit to delight in God will automatically call upon the Lord. The two go hand in hand. Someone who doesn't look at God with delight, who finds no reason or urge to praise God at all times, good or bad, will find it hard maintaining a strong prayer life.

Hindrance 5: *Getting weary of God*

> *'But thou hast not called upon me, O Jacob; but thou hast been weary of me.'* (Isaiah 43:22)

Sometimes when people pray for a long period over an issue and they don't get results, they think God must have given up on them. I've heard people say that God has given up on their nations and so they've stopped praying. Brethren, God never gives up on us. We must never get weary of praying. No matter how long it takes or how bleak the situation, we must keep praying. Surely God doesn't encourage us to pray in vain! There is a reward for all the time we put into prayer.

Example of Hannah

The story of Hannah in the Old Testament teaches the necessity of never growing weary, never giving up, always persisting. Hannah wanted a child so badly. The double portions and gifts her husband gave her could not satisfy her.

Year after year she kept going to the temple to pray with no results. She refused to give up. She pressed on. One day, 'Pastor' Eli found her praying and mistook her for a drunkard. Oh, that should have put her off, the holy high priest rebuking her! If it were today, as it is with some of our church people, she would have quarreled with the 'pastor', accusing him of not being filled with the Holy Spirit, not being anointed, etc. But Hannah humbled herself, submitted to spiritual authority and respectfully explained that she wasn't drunk but was pouring out her heart to the Lord. She was troubled. She needed a child. Pastor Eli understood, prayed with her and she got her miracle.

The enemy will try to discourage you, citing every possible reason why you should give up but don't you listen to him. Keep on keeping on. Pray until something happens.

Example of Jesus

Look at our Lord Himself in the garden of Gethsemane. There were enough reasons to make anyone give up on trying to keep praying. His prayer partners, Peter, James and John, failed to understand His situation. They failed to stand with Him in His hour of need. Twice He tried to wake them up to watch with Him but they kept on going right back to sleep. They couldn't watch with Him for even only one hour. (Incidentally, we learn from this story that the minimum time any believer is to spend in prayer every day is at least one hour.)

Despite failing to get prayer support from His colleagues, however, the Lord persisted. With strong cries and tears, He travailed before the only One who could save Him from death. (Some people say they don't want to express strong emotions in prayer, but the same people quite easily express a lot of emotion when angry!) The Lord wrestled on in prayer until He sweated blood. An angel came along to strengthen Him and He still kept on! Finally, He broke through. The battle was won. He had the victory. Nothing could destroy Him. It took persistence!

Hindrance 6: *Boredom and physical weariness*

I used to think that I am the only one who gets bored with prayer sometimes, not feeling like praying at all. Then I happened to read a book by David Yonggi Cho, the great Korean pastor. Dr Cho wrote that he too doesn't feel like praying always. I then realized that it happens to all people, even to the most spiritual and prayerful. In fact, even the great New Testament apostle, Paul, had problems too in his prayer life. I know it because he wrote in Romans 8:26 that the Spirit helps our infirmities. Note that he used the word 'our', implying that he too was included among those with infirmities in prayer.

There are days you wake up and you feel like no word of prayer is willing to come out of your mouth. You feel dry and bored. Do not let that make you shun prayer that day. We are to pray whether we feel like it or not. How can we obey the command to pray without ceasing if we are going to pray only when we feel like it?

You will not always feel like getting out of bed to pray but do it anyhow. Do not let the devil convince you to pray in bed. You will go back to sleep. Get out of bed and sit on a mat or a chair. Do something to make your body get out of the mood of sleep. Begin to pray slowly. If you feel like no words coming, begin to pray in tongues. If you are Spirit-filled, the tongues are always there. As you go on, you will find yourself being charged and ready to go.

Prayer works a lot like a car engine. First the engine has to be heated. You let it charge a little and after a while it is ready to go. Our flesh certainly does not want to pray; but pray we must! If you will begin, that flow will eventually come. And if you keep training yourself by being regular in prayer, the period for the flow to come will keep shortening. At first it may take you an hour or two to get into the flow. Later it may reduce to thirty minutes and finally to just a few minutes or even seconds.

Recently I returned home from an extended mission trip abroad. We had conducted prayer schools in England, France and Brazil. When I got back home I felt that I needed to rest, even from prayer. In the middle of the night my wife woke up to pray, as she usually does. I heard her praying but I told myself that I couldn't join her because I was physically too weary. Suddenly the Holy Spirit commanded me to get out of bed: there was a spirit of weariness on me. I obeyed and we had a great time in prayer!

You've got to be aggressive against physical weariness. Be violent. The kingdom of God is taken by force. Your body will tell you that you need your sleep. That may be true sometimes but I tell you that you need the presence of God more and that, my friend, means prayer!

Help from corporate prayer

Sometime back I used to talk with Brother John Mulinde about breaking through in prayer to the level of travailing, the level of prevailing. At that time, we didn't know what it was called. Later on we heard someone refer to it as breakthrough prayer. We began to teach our people. After three months testimonies began to trickle in. Some of the people were breaking through. First the prayer captains broke through and soon the entire church reached that level. There was travailing, wailing, groaning in every prayer meeting. That has remained the case up to today.

Holding hands

When in corporate prayer we hold one another's hands. This is a physical action but we have found it to be helpful as a point of contact to 'pull' those who have not yet broken through into the holy of holies. There is a transfer of anointing that happens as we hold hands. Remember, it is the anointing that breaks all yokes.

While it is true that your personal praying is really the measure of your prayer life, corporate prayer can be the means of pulling someone from outer court praying into inner court praying. Never depend on corporate prayer only. What you are in prayer alone is your true prayer life. But too, do not neglect corporate prayer. It can help you overcome that weariness. As you pray together with others, that corporate prayer anointing does something to you.

People come to our annual Africa Camp meeting from all over the world because they are hungry for God. Most of them enter a new spiritual realm during camp. One of the reasons for this is that by coming to camp, they change location and that helps them focus more clearly on their goal. The camp has the kind of atmosphere where people can separate themselves from the routine of their daily lives and concentrate on meeting with God.

The point is: do whatever is necessary to help you overcome weariness and boredom. Don't just sit there and moan about how you do not enjoy praying. Do something: come to the camp meeting or go to the Prayer Mountain or whatever.

Conclusion

Beloved, my prayer is that the thoughts I have shared in this book have stirred you to aspire to greater heights in your prayer life as well as in your general walk with God. God is no respecter of persons. Throughout history He has always answered the prayers of His people. The children of Israel in Egypt cried out to God and He sent them a deliverer in the person of Moses. During the days of Mordecai, the Jews called upon God and He wrought a mighty deliverance. There is no difference even today. He is still the God who answers prayer. We have seen Him do great things in Uganda, in answer to prayer. I have no doubt that He is willing to do similar things in other nations if only God's people will rise up and pray through to victory.